# Bruised Paradise

# Bruised Paradise

*Poems by Kevin Stein*

University of Illinois Press   *Urbana and Chicago*

Publication of this book was supported in part by a
grant from the Illinois Arts Council, a state agency.
© 1996 by Kevin Stein
Manufactured in the United States of America
P 6 5 4 3 2

*This book is printed on acid-free paper.*

Library of Congress Cataloging-in-Publication Data
Stein, Kevin, 1954–
Bruised paradise : poems / by Kevin Stein.
p.    cm.
ISBN 978-0-252-06537-8 (pbk. : alk. paper)
I. Title.
PS3569.T37139B75  1996
811'.54—dc20                        95-32545
                              CIP

# Acknowledgments

Some poems in this book have appeared previously. Grateful acknowledgment is made to the following magazines: "What Language Makes of Us," *Boulevard*; "Baseball Arrives in Richmond, Indiana" and "Human Commerce," *Indiana Review*; "Awaiting My Daughter's Suitor," "Benefit Picnic, Cigar Makers' Strike, 1884," "Black Bread," "Revenant," "In the Room with Seventeen Windows," "St. Andrew's Catholic Men's Choir, after Practice, at Blickwedel's Tavern and Grocery," and "Two Hungers," *The Missouri Review*; "Night Shift, after Drinking Dinner, Container Corporation of America, 1972" and "Seeds," *The North American Review*; "Body and Soul," *Poet & Critic*; "Authorial Distance," *Poetry*; "Broken Pines," "The First Performance of the Rock 'n' Roll Band *Puce Exit*," "The Presence of God in Our Lives," "Rooster Saved from the Soup Pot," and "World without End," *Poetry Northwest*; "Fathers," *Quarterly West*; "His Blue Period," "Past Midnight, My Daughter Awakened by Miles Davis' *Kind of Blue*," and "What Passes for Paradise," *Shenandoah*.

"First Performance of the Rock 'n' Roll Band *Puce Exit*," "Upon Finding a Black Woman's Door Sprayed with Swastikas, I Tell Her This Story of Hands," and "World without End" appeared in *Sweet Nothings: An Anthology of Rock and Roll in American Poetry* (Bloomington: Indiana University Press, 1994).

I'm grateful for the generous support of the National Endowment for the Arts and Bradley University's Research Excellence Committee, whose funds provided time to write some of these poems. For his sustaining friendship and thoughtful advice, special thanks is due Dean Young. I am also indebted to James Ballowe, Keith Ratzlaff, Michael Van Walleghen, Roger Mitchell, Ralph Burns, Jim Elledge, Philip Jones, and Dwight Brill. Thanks also to Demetrice, Geri, and Sarah, and most of all, as always, to Deb, who keeps the faith. Finally, I'm grateful for those family members, now all gone, who saved a few pieces of Bernard Liss's life and thus made me curious to imagine how he, my great-great-grandfather, might have lived the rest of it.

. . . to attend, singing, to the trace of the fugitive gods.

—MARTIN HEIDEGGER

We know and we understand, a mighty god is a living man.

—BOB MARLEY

*This book is for Deb, Kirsten, and Joseph.*

# Contents

# 1   This Furious Promise

# Past Midnight, My Daughter Awakened by Miles Davis' *Kind of Blue*

In the presence of blue, it's the eye
that signals to the brain that signals
to the heart, *slow down, slow down,*
a process of attenuation I hear
in Coltrane's notes, loping
then sprinting, then nearly gone,
Chambers' barely audible bass
holding sway amidst the fifties hiss.
It's then I think death must be like this,
its last beats sweeter because few,
the body closing doors and shutting windows,
locking up before the long buzz, crackle,
microphone hum. Then Miles and Cannonball
and Coltrane, horns whispering "So what,"
building in defiance until I wonder
at their swagger, their fear,
as I did at the woman in Jimmy's Bar,
who having nothing to lose, popped
the French heart medicine "experimental"
only tamely described. Quaffed them
with a Guinness, shoveled popcorn in,
and would not turn from those who stared.
Like me, birthday boy half in the bucket,
or those whose glass slipped from hand
to floor upon seeing her puffy face
the color of Franz Marc's horse. Still,
it's my mother's fault I can't think of blue
as forlorn: her kitchen and bath,
carpet and drapes, that starving goose
above her pale couch—all blue,

or better, some shade of calm embodied
by a thing we lounge upon, wash our hands in,
or do what we close the door to do in.
It's no miracle the sadness of the wretched
didn't come to mind studying the woman's
blue face, or watching the June delphinium
offer its trumpet of blossom in September,
horn of plenty, yellow throated surprise
as deft as my daughter, backlit
by stairwell light, hands on hips
in the manner young children take
with parents who've misbehaved.
Glancing at me, the chair I sit in,
our striped futon, even the cheap
Chagall taped to the wall, she says,
"I guess I'm doomed to love blue,"
a joke she knows will bring my laughter,
doomed to love what lifts and often
kills us—sailor's ocean, pilot's sky,
those eyes whose sheen I had not reckoned on.

# Night Shift, after Drinking Dinner,
## Container Corporation of America, 1972

Through the cheap iron gate and its mythic
irony (for who would storm and sack
a box-making plant?); down the cigarette-stained

hall and past the super's all-glass office,
I lurched and reeled and had, as the boys
who play the ponies say, to piss like a racehorse.

It wasn't the urinous light, puddled
and wavering as if a mirage in some
bad Abbott and Costello Sunday movie;

not the yawing and clanging, the squeal
of machines in heat, for reproducing,
after all, is their anointed duty;

not the scent of sulphur and hot glue,
those belching and farting fork lifts,
not even "death valley" steaming cardboard.

It was a raspy *Jesus Christ* I heard
above the six pack hiss (Pabst Blue Ribbon,
a buck sixty-nine, cold), a voice which beckoned

me to Shipping where acid-tripping Bill
had metal-strapped his finger to a pallet.
Efficient, even when stoned, he'd stencilled:

SHIP TO: PITTSBURGH, PA / HEINZ 57
200 COUNT / SCORED / DOUBLE-NOTCHED.
That, my introduction to LSD and political subversion,

5

so little of either in my GM town:
alternators, headlamps, the domino theory,
"An Okie from Muskogee" our jukebox anthem.

What I knew of war I got from Cronkite's
daily tally, each lurid tone of death
on camera, that Vietnamese girl napalmed

and naked. This was what I watched —
mind you, watched, and took to saying "peace"
instead of good-bye, easy enough if your draft

number's 185. So it was when oh so wild Bill
lifted the stub to his lips and sucked it
as he would a paper cut, *Mr. Natural's*

*going to keep me out of 'Nam*, he said,
which meant: would keep him whole,
notwithstanding the lopped-off index finger;

which meant: no trigger, no Uncle Sam
poking his chest. He laughed
the bellyful laugh of shock,

the giddy electric giggle of lysergic acid.
We pried his finger from the skid,
buried it in a cup of ice, our ship

of state scuttled in rose waters.
There was beauty in the mind's eye,
which could afford to be inconsolably

clumsy with facts. "Keep on Truckin',"
said the little blotter acid man —
his boots huge, arm raised, finger pointed

to some constellation of loss
and promised rebirth. There was
irony, too, in our rush to hide the cup,

red-faced paramedics screaming,
"Where is it, man?"—how cleaving
may cleave a part unto the whole.

# First Performance of the Rock 'n' Roll Band *Puce Exit*

If puce were sound not color,
　　it would be us: Deep Purple,
though more confused and discordant,

our guitars tuned in electric ignorance
　　of tone, key, each other—the word
*puce* derived from the Latin for "flea,"

as appropriate for pests in the hides
　　of neighbors—our raucous weekend practice,
pubescent groupies lingering on basement steps,

first on the block to show hearing loss,
　　first to wear paisley with polka dots.
And *exit*, of course, because music is

our ticket out. It's Peggy Wasylenski's
　　fourteenth birthday party, a real gig,
her parents too cool, or simply so new

to America they're expecting something
　　with accordion and banjo, not the freight
we unload from my father's blue Chevy:

amps, mikes, drums, Christmas color wheels
　　for visual effect. We set up in the dirt
floor garage, our amps a wall of sound

maybe knee high across the left bay.
　　Everything's plugged into a quad outlet
above the single ceiling bulb. Orange wires

cascade around us like a waterfall
    of blown fuses. We start, start over,
and start again, until we get right

the three drumstick beat and launch into
    an 18 minute version of "Satisfaction."
I'm howling "I can't get no!" even though,

in eighth grade, I'm not sure what it is
    I can't get any of, but it's something,
I am sure, I need as badly as any guy

ever needed anything, like "voice lessons,"
    the drummer screams. On break, we play
spin the bottle, Peggy flicking her tongue

and me choking with surprise, with glee,
    with adolescent resolve to improve
on the next round, which never comes.

Police arrive to pull the knotted plug
    and send us scurrying for the bushes,
guitars around our necks, though no one

is drunk or stoned on anything other than
    the rush of innocence soon to take a turn,
accelerating around the corner like Peggy,

three years later, first night with license
    and the family station wagon, her eyes
on the lit radio dial and not on the barber,

my barber, trudging home in rain, the scissors
    in his breast pocket soon to puncture
his heart beneath her tire's worn tread.

But none of that has happened to happen.
　　It's spring, and the bushes we hunker in
make riotous bloom. They smell of sachet,

cheap pink tins scenting my mother's floral
　　dressing table. Or maybe it's Peggy,
her breath against my still whiskerless face,

cops' flashlights, cymbals hissing as they spill
　　in puffs of dust, and neither of us
in a hurry to leaven this sweet bouquet.

# Broken Pines

*Susurrus* is a word I've had to learn
   the hard way, as when fact insinuates
meaning through boughs of pines I climbed

ten years ago, all of them now wind-raked
   and fallen, broken above the waist like those
spindly women who roam the nursing home

where my mother bakes cakes and pies and cookies.
   She dresses in white. She wears a beaded hairnet.
Some nights, I'll lug the basket of treats

from hall to darkened hall, so she can hug
   the beagle-faced boy, the girl with pretzeled
limbs, all the pale-eyed residents of God's

waiting room who laugh and squeal and wheeze
   in my mother's skinny arms. For this,
she makes four dollars an hour. Cherry pies

and pumpkin cupcakes, gingerbread men with
   cinnamon eyes, these scent the place—
as do urine and vomit, the mix as fragrant

as the breath of the soon-gone who motions
   your ear down close and rasps, "It's time."
If this were rock 'n' roll, now would come

the blessed hush of thunderous drums,
   the splash and shoosh of cymbals,
maybe a guitar's icy tinkling—segue

to some personal exposition sure to make
    cash enough to soothe anyone's black leather
despair. It's only this furious promise

of rain lashing white pines, my uncle
    asking for Basie or Ellington, something
with swing to it, though he can't dance,

his body made Jell-O by muscular dystrophy,
    as were his father, his brother, his third son.
I bend to empty the bedpan. He whispers

in my blue ear, bruised and hideous
    from a southside pickup game, warning
my mother's a carrier, I could be next.

Sure, what passes on I've absorbed
    from her like music during sleep.
Sure, I ought to say, those are the odds,

though I say nothing. Not because I'm brave
    or angry or too guilty to speak.
Not because I model self-restraint.

Just because it's her I'm thinking of,
    how she tends the flushed and wilted
with brushed velvet compassion —

that word meaning to bless another body
    as if it were your soul. Because
I'm wrong. It's her song not his,

rising above Basie's "Oh, Lady Be Good,"
    its chorus plush with scotch pines
and wheelchaired children, all whisper and sigh.

# Poem for Tomas and
## the Red-Haired Girl with Asters

When he thinks his mother's come to strum
    her knuckles across the window glass
as call to prayer, it's only sparrows
    in eaves and gutters, the sibilant clamor
of nestlings' first flight that bolts him

from the chair to yank the curtain back
    and face his own face so wavering
in the day's last pilferings of light
    the yard's rose of Sharon blooms then grays
atop his head. In dream he'd forgotten

her death. In dream he was 16
    in Stalin Square, hoisting himself
by the statue's great pants pockets
    to wrap cable around its waist
while Budapest catalyzed itself

beneath him, the climate so electric
    he imagined himself heir to clerics
who'd rung church bells during storms
    and danced lightning's quick two step
with a rope. That's why he lingered there

in '56, above the photographer's hail
    of flashes, lingered even as Stalin lurched
his first few inches toward wet cobblestone.
    This, he tells me from an oak's low branches,
too late and probably too drunk to be in a tree,

at the end of a workshop I led, though
    to where and for what end I'm not sure,
as he climbs higher to show me, "Here.
    This high. I was this high," hands above
his head like the part in "Eensty Weensty Spider"

when the sun comes out to dry up all
    the rain. That's why, he says, when Stalin
lay prostrate, only his boots upright,
    he scrambled up the left to spit inside,
and had no need for red wine passed from hand

to hand or women's full-mouthed kisses,
    though he did accept a fist of asters
from a red-haired girl who curtsied
    and danced away in song. Now past midnight,
campus bells clang, thunder booms above

the buttoned-down homes of Normal, Illinois,
    but Tomas won't climb down the oak
because his mother had come to haul him
    home that day, and when he'd refused,
had swung her scarf around his neck

to drag him off to dinner of lamb
    and new potatoes because she knew
there'd be few more like it. Dinner
    while others stormed the radio station
and soldiers thrust rifles at girls

who only sang louder. Dinner because
    the redhead's asters did not deflect
a single bayonet. That's why this story within
    a story within a story, told, as promised,
so Tomas would clamber down among the living.

# What Language Makes of Us

Habit makes him put     music on
she can't hear,     although she lays
her hands upon a     speaker to feel
the first thrust     of Mozart's 29th
vibrate like her     satisfied cat.
That morning     they'd walked among
the lilies in     late bloom, gold cups
raised above     October's astonished dross,
the scene     so clustered with
surprise     she'd bent each word around
her tongue     and he'd only frowned,
covered her     lips with his, embarrassed
for her, though     she wasn't. It's after lunch
so he pours Dewar's     that goes untouched,
glass beading sweat     as they make love,
sweating, on the black     leather couch,
a red pillow propped     beneath her
so shoulders and knees     squeak their silken
leather rhythm. He'd     asked her to sign
"yes, yes" or "more,"     something to say
he's doing all right,     as if without words
there'd be no way of     knowing. How can she?
Why? Her hands speak     language he has no
trouble with, her moans     those of any woman,
though musically slurred     like a 45 played
at 33 rpm. Because she's     deaf, he says things
he never had while making     love, alternately
genteel and foul. She cracks     her lids
just wide enough to read his     lips and thus
conducts her own arrangement.     She holds her hands
on his throat and chest to feel     their music

strummed wilder than Mozart's.      It's symphony
for hand and eye she plays.      He wants to tell her
when he's reached the point of      no return,
but signing, his fingers lock      and his tongue, too,
so his struggle brings its      blessing and curse,
plural as sex, and what      comes from his throat
wrenches free of language,      taking him with it.
A word? No, nothing she'd      read on anyone's lips,
a creaking she felt but didn't      hear, some colossal
gate unhinged for purple-robed      priests to march through,
torches high, and bid him welcome      to her kingdom.

# Fathers

I don't look like my father,
kneeling before the lit dial
of the radio he knelt before
when, prayerful as the altar boy
he was and wasn't, he tuned
the RCA's seven bands past all
the shows worth listening to
to the staticky dispensation
of ship's communications,
another world collapsed
tired and worn into his lap.
His family saved things.
He saved only this: reliquary
of words he doesn't believe in
as he did that morning
his mother came to him,
her hands ablossom with hankies,
eyes dewy as they always were
when the bougainvillea offered
their dollops of color,
the proud shasta and coreopsis,
her bedroom window trellised
with red trumpet creeper
and the tiny angelic strumming
of hummingbird wings.
I won't worry the way he did
that she'd found his French
playing cards, women in lingerie
reclined on couches, leaned
against a tree, or his favorite,
Ace of Hearts, bent over

a wingback chair and showing
just a blush of breast
an artist had pinked in
with enough deftness to give
his first thickening and rise,
which in twenty years
gave rise to two daughters,
two miscarried, me. I can't
hear the same crackle and hiss,
her shuffling steps and that pause—
her breath like slivers of glass
drawn and held—before she said
his father had bled to death
in line hungry for work,
ulcers ruptured like an earthen dam,
and with no phone, a stranger
had to knock to tell her
the boys did all they could.
I can't feel what he felt,
child of Depression economics,
forced thereafter to share
his room with a grandmother
who'd survived rheumatic fever
but could not bear for him
to see her bald head, asking
him each night to pillow his face
before she draped her wig
across an upturned pitcher's skull,
handle protruding like a nose.
I don't even know what he knows
of this radio, though I watch him
spin dials and flip switches with a style
I should pay attention to.
By sleight of hand, he pulls in
ships at sea: French, Russian,

then the Japanese he liked best
as a boy, its exotic clucks and twangs
so otherworldly he'd pretend
it was his father speaking to him
heaven's indecipherable language,
every phrase alive with promise.
In the radio's burnt orange glow,
he mouths words he practiced then,
and used, ten years later,
on the bomb-dimpled island of Attu,
the battle a clearing of bunkers
and revetments, tundra wet enough to pool
the bootprints of those who'd run,
their steps a shimmering, inch-deep
chain of lakes he had only to follow.
"Come home," he'd say, "to wife,
daughters, sons," his Japanese
singsong in the sulfurous air.

# Upon Finding a Black Woman's Door Sprayed with Swastikas, I Tell Her This Story of Hands

How to tell you hate was in rancorous bloom,
    spiking my town's tepid breath
with florets of white sheets & raised,
    gloved fists. How to say we seethed
around our school, white & black splayed

on either side of Lincoln Street, its broken
    promise. Tick, tick, tick, & I was late
for chemistry, prelude to explosion
    as flushed & spontaneous as any combustion
you'd swear won't happen, fists & chains

catalyzing our frothy breath. I screamed
    "Be cool, man!" beneath a pitiful catalpa,
beneath its blossoms the Creek called *kutuhlpa*,
    "head with wings," though some of us
had surely lost our heads & any chance

of flight. I screamed "Peace!"
    & took a punch in my white face.
After the sirens & nightsticks, after
    snarling dogs & the midmorning spritz
of Mace, after the curses & bloody lips,

we felt exotic, lured to some fine madness
    we'd never recover from. What I had
in mind involved my girlfriend, not Clayton
    thumbing a ride, huge defensive end
who'd trashed halfbacks as he lilted

"Going to a Go Go" & I piled on. His black
    hand swallowed mine, his knuckles bruised,
bleeding. We didn't say "brother." We didn't
    sing of slain Jack & Bobby & Martin.
We didn't swear we loved this life, either—

the woof & warp of hour upon hour tottering
    like a palace of the lost, beguiled,
misbegotten. It wasn't exactly cruising,
    though we drove windows down, AM 1470
spooning out Smokey Robinson & the Miracles,

their honeyed voices as smooth as
    my parents' powder blue Bel-Air.
How to say I felt spring waft its redolent
    insistence across the cracked dash
as I harmonized with Bill "Smokey" Robinson.

How to tell you Clayton's hand daubed
    my split lip with iodine, all the while
a bloody sunset reeled in the night:
    fish of dark, fish of peace, speckled fish
of forgiveness he knew more of than I.

# The Presence of God in Our Lives

Blessed would describe the ride
    we took that night Allan wondered
what speed could leave behind,
    smoking fat pink joints he scored
from Bible-plant master printers
    so stoned even the Book of Genesis

lost its place, befuddled
    by a fog of dinnertime smoke,
our world lurched into being
    from nothingness. Let me explain.
He carried a verse torn from
    Ecclesiastes, which the Byrds turned

pop lyric, believing there was
    "a season for every purpose under
heaven"—until he met the Vietnamese
    woman whose drunken vet husband
tied her to their bed and waved
    his buddies in. "It's a party,"

he said, giving Allan first dibs,
    who untied and dressed her,
bought her breakfast at Waffle House.
    He night-managed King's Inn, and so
could slip her the key to a room
    some cross-country trucker had vacated:

free cable, clean linen, Bible study
    on TV. Allan fell in love.
On Christmas Eve, the Bible told her

to save her husband from perdition,
and she went home. We watched
    her turn the key, lift the curtain

to say "I'm okay," then burned
    a block's worth of cold rubber,
a language we understood to mean
    get by, get over, and step on it,
all of which came to mind
    when the New York Central wailed

its baleful note, its unforgiving cyclops
    bearing anger equal to his,
though slower and less blessed,
    by God, this once. Airborne,
we came to rest in a stubble field,
    snow quilting the car like a blanket

of the dispossessed. Our angels
    folded their wings and slept.
Those unlucky ones, wafting over
    the black-haired woman we'd left
behind, plucked "O Holy Night"
    on their starry harps, and wept.

# His Blue Period

He asks the questions and they reply, hang up
the phone, or blurt impossibly crude responses
to the survey's "Would you like to test,
free of charge, a new toilet tissue product?"

He takes it with a smile, though unnecessarily
(for who can see?), if only because each
hour buys more paint: more cadmium yellow
and rich magenta, more neon green of April

maple leaves, and who knows when he'll enter
his blue period—think of all the cash
for layer upon layer of that. What's more,
it's work he doesn't have to shave

or cut his hair for, wear boots not spackled
with paint—just showers and clean clothes
in fear of the inevitable June of broken
air conditioning, thirty-six people

in a bathtub-sized room, and no windows
to let in Peoria's tepid distractions.
Last month, voices on the other end
rated Massachusetts health care

and gas station restrooms, or reasoned
the most insidious causes for not flossing
after meals. He checked appropriate boxes,
wrote brief notes half asleep in the buzz

of language like bees about the hive,
the words sated and stingerless. This week
it's breast cancer, family histories
and tears glinting on faces he can't see

and wouldn't recognize if he did,
all of it ending with request for patient
self-examination: phone set down with
a clunk, ruffling cotton or chemise

or sometimes, surely, silk; that thwack
of bra strap and the humorless possibility
the voice belongs to a body where something
invasive harbors its self-destructive self

in the small or sagging or voluminous breasts
of someone brunette or blonde, dark-skinned
or light, someone with children in diapers
or children in the grave, someone life is having

its sweetly vacant way with. Until his call.
Then *poof*, they're searching the locale of every
man's slack-jawed curiosity and graceless lust,
hoping not to find what they're looking for.

In the muffled, fiber optic silence,
he's thinking titanium white will brighten
the painting on his easel; he's thinking
geodes and their hollowed-out crystalline

surprise, how he'll brush that sparkle
into the eyes of his Madonna and child,
as if she were crying at the thought
of what sacred life she cups in her hands.

# Revenant

That March the factory axed me, a neighbor
unclinched my fists with his shovel's consolation.
We planted hardy quince and potentilla,
juniper and the delicate flowering crab.
No, not *we* — I dug their bottomless holes
and grunted each into its appointed place
until his iced-tea-eye winked, *there*.
Bent on knee, I sorted music from static
on the Ford's old Philco, AM crackling
with distant storms, Da Nang's body count,
a slew of acid-induced rock 'n' roll hymns
to the revolution he despised.
We hardly talked — my jaw clamped with
Seventies' anger, his because mine was —
so the joyless task was left to his wife,
flushed-cheeked from peach wine,
to kitchen-corner me with the story
of a boy hidden the day his parents were boxed
to Auschwitz. The false wall, the woman's hand
that brought cold soup, his piss pot
and that single candle. All this,
because he cried amidst bloodred tulips
with black eyes and I'd asked *why*.
The innocent *why* sure to bring on trouble,
the *why* I nailed to the wall this morning
while framing my son's new room.
You know what happens. It's a day like any
other, then a child falls from a fickle oak,
the dog at last surprises a squirrel,
your father calls to say he's misplaced
his good teeth. A day like any other,

the story goes, until the wall you've built
walls off a face lit by candlelight:
a boy on his knees beside the low slot
soup bowls slide through. You close your eyes,
or shutter them with gloved hands,
hoping the vision will flee, and still
it blooms: red tulips with black eyes,
red without. You've seen enough to know
who clutches the soup, whose lips kiss and kiss
the mottled wrist: your neighbor, your son,
never you.

# World without End

Before my brother-in-law lost his telephone job
    to the first recession
a brief war wouldn't cure, he worked alone
    200 feet beneath
the humpbacked hills of Southern Indiana,

tending AT & T fiber optics, and as unexpected bonus,
    two obsolete coaxial cables
linking both coasts to some hard rock Colorado
    mountain sanctuary,
where blips adorn a panoply of mint green screens

and everyone wears headphones, though the jamming
    they listen to
isn't music to anyone's ears. Among clay and the muzzles
    of brown-spotted cattle,
his site was bomb proofed—replete with freeze-dried stew,

bottled water, backup diesel generators and a score
    of acid batteries
to back up those, and shiny silver suits with gloves
    supple enough
to squeeze an M-16's trigger on the irradiated masses.

"A link in the Armageddon line," he called it,
    brutal with humor,
and don't start now with your moral imperatives.
    It was work,
twenty-three years better than Arkansas sharecropping

that broke his parents, even their mules too swaybacked
     to auction off,
and who could feed two hay-hungry pets? Before he shot
     those mules,
he took the instamatic photograph he's taped to his

gray metal desk, underground, 194 feet deeper than where
     they lay.
It's the photo we go retrieve, his last day, a bit drunk,
     rain emptying the sky
as if it had no intention of stopping there: soon

the ozone-depleted atmosphere, next the moon, perhaps
     a skein of stars
who'd corroborate the luckless Chicken Little, and then
     the sun itself,
shrunken into the pinprick of borrowed light

his miner's cap pokes through elevator dark. Slow,
     chilled ride.
We lower as if hand over hand into the room's incessant,
     denture-like clacking:
each raised receiver, each dial tone, each good-bye, so long,

click. "Yes, I'll wear my black dress, black pumps
     and sequined shawl."
"Have you heard about . . . ," "and mother always . . . ,"
     "No, I said. No."
How do I explain my urge to listen, my appetite for love

and anger that's not mine? Or worse, my yearning to pull
     the plug,
prompt the plural shaking of heads in hallways and kitchens,
     a plangent chorus
of "Hello, hello? . . ." —or safe below a rock shelf

the first anxious "We've lost them, sir," the scurrying
  and alarms,
a dream of missiles like rain from purple clouds, and then
  that haunted cloud,
the shape of fear sauteed in a pan of ignorance,

served with lunch. But the cold war's over,
  and thankfully
my brother-in-law has switched on the radio he wired
  down the shaft,
against all company regulations. It's tuned to oldies,

and I half-expect Sha Na Na's obnoxious "Get a Job,"
  for irony's sake.
It's Van Morrison, instead, his group Them doing
  the original version
of "Gloria," Van punctuating the "i" with fists in the gut.

We dance, play air guitar, both of us blue-haloed
  by banks of lights
installed to counter Seasonal Affective Disorder.
  Who could be sad,
dear reader, in such a state of grace? Buried in earth,

a grand reconciliation taking place around us,
  entombed with music—
if not of the spheres—then of voices speaking,
  listeners listening,
and hope, our sturdy friend, solid as two good mules.

# In the Room with Seventeen Windows

A surprise child, born in their forties,
had pushed them into this room among the oaks
whose twice-trimmed branches still caressed
the house with a snare drummer's brushed *shoosh*.

A room so new she'd awaken and stumble
to the walk-in closet to squat on a john
that wasn't beneath her. He'd hear the thump
and her cursing, then reach for the switch

he'd wired too far from the bed.
This time a storm thrashed south of town,
so the sky strobed black to white to black,
as when a child he'd so furiously flicked

the light switch — while his babysitter
frugged to *Meet the Beatles* — his pleasure
had worn it out. No click, no light.
Maybe that's what made him want to make love,

something conditioned into him that night,
or something hardwired all along
and thus something genetic he was slave to:
a thought which comforted him as he kissed

her neck and shoulders. She lay still,
eyes focused somewhere in the universe
above his face, "What's that sound,"
she asked, "something sawing itself in half?"

The katydid, enticing a mate, ratcheted
so passionately their room's bare walls
reverberated with its frantic cranking.
She couldn't concentrate, imagining

the thing on a branch looking in
one of seventeen windows. Watching.
She made him flip on the deck light,
thinking that would shut it up. Then

a broom to flail low branches and scare it
off: he in boxers and Birkenstocks,
grass wet, the sky light-switching above,
rainwater showering him with each broom swipe.

Still the katydid sang its anthem,
insistent, hopeful, and imploring,
a tune which, given his own predicament,
reminded him that daily four people

call Graceland and ask to speak to Elvis.
Seriously. No one needed to tell him
love was irrational, a lascivious joke
of the gods, so why not—he bent on knee

and sang "Love Me Tender" through the screen,
just reaching the first plaintive
". . . never let me go" as her alarm buzzed
and the katydid, resigned to fate, hushed.

# Seeds

It came as a gift comes
on a day not your birthday,
came mingled with surprise
and asking to be *cherished*
as one would if British
or a hopeless romantic
like that girl whose father
was the guitar-playing sheriff
who earned his black belt
busting bricks and singing
on the Grand Ole Opry
before a crowd as astonished
as I was at 19, hormonal wreck
not smart enough to keep it
in my pants, for she was beguiling
in the station wagon with TOP COP
license plates, all violins and candles,
lilting Italian opera she'd heard
sleeping beneath white taffeta
and the moon beyond the mesh-windowed
jailhouse where her family lived
in quarters as posh as Madison County
could afford, French poodle and all,
where prisoners scraped tin cups
along bars as in a black and white
and she thought to disappear
as wholly as our child she aborted,
only a puff of smoke to quell
the dull fires of the heart,
that fickle organ all things return to,
penitent, seeking the replenishment

my hand chanced upon this morning
while retrieving my daughter's ball,
finding instead the bristled shafts
of raspberries hidden from jays,
berries so ripe we knelt in grass
and ate our fill, my wife spilling
from the black bathing suit whose straps
would not stay put, all the world suspended
in the oceans of her eyes, blue
swimming with light in the browned out
prairie of Sunday noon and oaks
with arms raised in prayer.
It came to me then, kneeling beside
the woman I know enough to cherish.
Came as rain from clear sky,
as music sifting a wall,
miraculous piano, bass, and snare.
Came tasting of salt on the lips
of God or your beloved,
the long day spilling into
long night. It came as plush
as velvet or cheap velours,
the pillow propped beneath
a waiting lover, bedroom
as green as the towel tossed
over a lamp. It came with fingers
purpled and redolent of jam,
this sweet abandon whose kiss
tastes faintly of ash.

# God's Mailman

His purgatory is to learn what he never learned
    among us, we of breast and thigh and buttocks.
That test he failed first day on job,

smudging the swimsuit issue and with it
    Elle McPherson's ample bosom, which The Hand
had made and knew was good—though wrong

to look upon. His punishment: a watch dog
    to see he doesn't peek and she's no angel.
He strokes her ear, black as midnight over Malta.

Her tail loops the air. She gnaws the Holy Mail Box,
    gold softer than the hickory stick she fetched
amidst prairie grass, near the river bending

its muddy elbow through Peoria. She'd like
    to circle the girl floating on a raft,
blonde hair haloed in sun's glint. She'd like

to bark the bowlegged meterman to such submission
    his treats are bribes to pass the fence.
She'd love to nap beside the wood stove,

chase squirrels, roll in some good dead thing.
    Who wouldn't? Who'd prefer to walk on air?
Now she watches, every minute of every blessed day,

as God's mailman rings the bell and waits
    on the purgatory of knees for The Hand
whose careful nails shine like sunrise over Malta,

light terrible as toothache, though they mustn't squint:
   pain a measure of atonement. She wags and wags,
nudges The Hand, squeezes her thick belly halfway

through those shimmering gates. She won't sit
   upon command, adding months to their solemn penance.
God's mailman scratches her ear, tastes her breath

as piquant as garden dirt. He looks for a stick,
   and finding none, tosses his crucifix instead,
convinced the price is worth her earthy company.

# What Passes for Paradise

begins with *good morning* spoken in a voice
a man could fall in love with on the phone —
its huskiness swirled with honey and promises
of honey — which becomes, by noon, the voice
a man can't live with, that *there, there, now*
a mother takes with the son who's launched
a line drive through Mrs. Wilson's picture window,
afternoon shattered like applause upon her
oriental carpet. This is the way of it,
as is my coming baldness, reading the *Times*

in bed, the long Sundays of rake and burn.
This lesson a friend learned, driving his
father's car home from the funeral, pulling
over and flagging me down to say he couldn't
bear to drive that car, "It's him I smell."
So we switched: I got cigars and rosewater,
he got my sour milk, french fries, diapers.
It was then I felt like the hermit crab
slipping on his new shell — the view's the same
but the steering's different, the clutch

too tight, all the radio pre-sets tuned
to country & western. What is it we love
about the familiar, the here and now always
on hand like the work gloves so well worn
they keep your hands' shape even when empty?
I thought I had an answer, after Brokaw
announced a comet would crush the earth
in 134 years and my daughter came to me
in tears. I'd begun the usual disquisition
on Heraclitean flux, on theory and hoax,

before I noticed the cheap atomizer
in her hand and the fragrance about her face,
before she blurted, "It's like a fish swam
in my eyes and left its sparkles." Water
and rinse, water and rinse, flushing the way
our bodies refuse what is not their own,
the slow cleansing rest can bring to a child's
first "Evening in Paris," her head still
scented upon the pillow's good night kiss.
It's times like this I wish for some simple

turning Galileo missed amidst the moons
of Jupiter, some equation Einstein let fall
from his pocket when reaching for the door key,
something to make me as bold as Robert Johnson
in 1826, ascending Salem's courthouse steps
with a bushel basket, a throng spread around
to witness his suicide by tomato,
the love apple thought poisonous by fools.
Who hasn't wished for the courage to raise
death to our pursed lips (a band playing

the funeral march, our doctor imploring
us please stop), to take the bite that prompts
heaving piles of men and women to faint?
To walk home, two dozen later, healthier
than before, threatened only by diarrhea.
It's a kind of knowing we're after, each
tessera glued in place so our angels
have two wings, two eyes, those hands reaching
down for us. It's a way to make do
we're looking for, some angle to forfend

the apocalyptic comet cruising our way
with universal charm. What do we get?

A day that begins with honey and becomes
a man dressed in the habiliments of
autumn, on his knees to September frost
that surprised even the careful gardener
he is not. What begins with promise comes
to this cracked vase of frost-singed roses
dropping petals among the dirty dishes,
the sink shimmering its stainless steel smile,

and this all we need of paradise.

# 2   On Blue Paper

*Historical sense and poetic sense should not, in the end,*
*be contradictory, for if poetry is the little myth we make, history*
*is the big myth we live, and in our living, constantly remake.*
  —ROBERT PENN WARREN

*Bernard Liss (1817–89), left Lengerich, Hanover, in what is now northern Germany, at the height of the 1845 potato famine. A late blight had devastated the potato crop from Ireland to Silesia in eastern Germany, depriving the working class of their staple food. Arriving in Baltimore with his wife Mary Angela, Liss followed the National Road west, lured by its promise of work and open land, pausing for a while in Cincinnati and eventually settling in Richmond, Indiana, in 1853. Due largely to commerce attracted by the Road, Richmond was then evolving into a bustling manufacturing and transportation center, and his carpentry skills were in great demand. There he and his wife built a house (which still stands), raised five children, died, and were buried.*

*A small bundle of his personal papers survives, and direct quotations from them appear in some of these poems.*

# Two Hungers

## 1. *Great Famine, 1845*

Never one for portents or signs,
the little clues the world flaunts
before our inattentive eyes,
I hardly noticed the surfeit
of flies, the finely polished wealth

of shimmering wings—even their
drone a low moan my ear became
accustomed to, the way those
who care for the dying seldom
note a man's last hard-won breath.

By autumn, our globe was a badly
bruised pear the bees had done with,
beset with flies!—though it wasn't
fruit they were after but potatoes
rotting in heaps in every

garden plot or field of Hanover.
The rains brought late blight, white mold
jacketing the undersides of leaves,
and below, thin-skinned sacks of mush,
useless flesh gone the way of all flesh.

## 2. *Proposal*

It wasn't the hunger made me ask,
though it was appetite nonetheless.
In six months, enough of us had died

the gravediggers hired help and paid
cash for new shovels. I didn't

want to starve to death never having
had a woman, God bless my soul.
When I went to Mary Angela,
she was dressed in her best black frock,
hair pinched tight, pinned and adorned

with her mother's only lace. She
already knew! I asked her how.
"It's just my shoes had come untied,"
she said, "and kept coming untied
all week. Mother says it's sure sign

I'll be asked to marry." She said
yes before I got the chance. I felt
like the greedy child who comes upon
his hidden birthday gift: that blush
of animal joy tinged with lost surprise.

# Black Bread

Oh honeyed sluice to paradise—the one
I'd dreamt of on sweltering afternoons,
tools slung across my back, sizing a casket
for the dead, fitting a table for the near-
dead who had no money and paid in bread,

which seemed insane to me, for who needs
a table when there's nothing but elbows
to put on it?—that slide to peace began
without the giddy rush I'd expected,
the fierce holiness of vengeful angels

singing, "We're free, and sailing to America!"
It didn't feel like freedom to camp, hungry
and dirty, on a Bremerhaven dock,
to be seventy-sixth and -seventh in line
for the *Anna Marie*, cargo ship bound

for Baltimore. But then, how could I know
what freedom felt like, never having been free?

    *    *    *

With the proper coin, I'd have bribed the ship's
clerk to get on board before the dry berths
were taken. I had none. We were bound
to get wet, and did. I'd saved a tin of pitch
from the last casket I'd sealed, and we smeared

black globs where timbers spouted sea water
with each heave and toss. Stacked along the ship's
flanks like boxes, the upper berths kept dry

and free of rats. Not ours. At night, I'd envy
each pair of shoes mounting the rope ladder,

then the other mounting: grunting lovers
who could not wait six weeks for a suitable bed,
four walls, a door that locked. I wondered
if the ship's constant rocking were hindrance
or help, and thought to find out for myself.

But my wife was not as curious as I,
and instead I'd lie in salty puddles,
imagining the creatures who watched us
pass above them: big-eyed, toothy,
cold-blooded and hungry as us, patiently

awaiting the worm wood to spill me into
their jaws. It made me strangely at home.

      *    *    *

A gaggle of toughs had snuck on liquor.
Drunk, and randy from weeks at sea, they'd pinch
our daughters and eye the wives, then piss
wherever they wanted. I had an axe, a hatchet,
and I'd have lopped theirs off, if need be;

they kept their distance. Every inch reeked
of their piss, of Virginia tobacco
surely harvested by slaves, like the dark-skinned
one attending the ship's captain. Age ten
or twelve, he gave a face to the faceless

mass I imagined bent at the waist in a field,
culling the crop unloaded at Bremerhaven.
He was the first Negro slave I'd seen.
In a squall, all of us confined below,
I'd swear their pungent sweat mingled with ours.

At first, I'd barter for cigars of the sweet stuff.
Then stench, and the slave's eyes, cured that vice.

                *     *     *

In candlelight, it's said even the grave
looks hospitable. So it was for us,
our cramped universe awash with golden,
almost precious light, the black bread I'd gotten
in payment spread on a wool blanket.

"Take this and eat of it," the Lord said,
a lesson I thought of each meal we ate —
that, and the notion it was His last supper
and might well be ours. We couldn't eat
the Bible, after all, and paper was all

I had in my pocket, the passport describing
a *28 year old, standing 5 feet, 7 zoll,*
*of stocky build, blond hair, blue eyes,*
but not the why and wherefore of love,
not the wrenched gut of a man leaving home,

not the least stone of a path bordered
by flowers, the door it led to, the bed within —
only the *somewhat bent nose, ordinary mouth*
*with good teeth, the quarter-moon scar on the thumb*
*of the left hand, a citizen of Hanover*

*who's married, free of symptoms of syphilis,*
*who speaks Platt-Deutsch and does not stutter.*

# Human Commerce

Always the wagons, loaded-down, tarped,
    domed-over, or open to foul weather,
always the faint rumble of an empty stomach,
    always the plain-faced hunger:

more linen, more wallpaper and tablecloths,
    more lamps and oil to burn in them,
more high-stitched boots and broadcloth,
    candlesticks and fine knives for home,

or woods, or tobacco house, for tavern
    or dimly lit street; always the wagons
and their thirsty, dust-caked teamsters
    spilling America's appetite westward

along the National Road, always the *wants*
    of those whose *needs* have been met
beyond old world dreams, these I join
    each day, hauling my own load of lumber,

hammer, and saw, to adorn the homes
    of bankers and merchants with oaken cabinets
and stairs that will not creak, offering
    my eldest daughter to cook and clean

and tend the pale children for a fee
    I'll keep half of as dowry and she the rest
for dresses, a new corset, some scented oil —
    all of it carried along that road I crossed

last night, traffic slowed by the slight reach
    of lantern light, when a man bid me stop.
His load had shifted, rotten planks had split,
    and now danger of losing everything.

Shucking my coat, I crawled beneath the wagon,
    lifted my lantern, and saw his cargo:
so many black arms and legs and faces
    I thought he carried the dead South

to rendering. Startled, I knew what's said
    about their eyes at night was true—
a dozen pairs of stars looked through me
    to my soul, searing it with their fear.

I did not move. I did not say a word.
    I was thinking of yesterday's *Daily Item*,
how a Negro had gazed into blue eyes,
    and she into his, with such intention

the sheet music had spilled from her arms,
    raising a red cloud of dust. Offering
her the sheets, his hand had brushed her breast
    and she'd held it there an instant

before her father bellowed across the street,
    and the Negro ran, was hunted down, lynched.
Though not before the scalping, disembowelment
    and the blue belt his insides made wrapped

around his waist, not before his genitals
    were fed to the dogs who'd tracked him.
I did not move. I did not say a word.
    King William had taught me a lesson

about birthright as arbitrary as color
    and soulless as Hanover in 1845.
The driver's face loomed above me,
    white and round as the moon over any man,

free or not. "Can you fix it?"
    I refused, not wanting to dirty my hands
with him, his pitiful cargo. "What's
    your name? I'll send you payment

when we arrive at Levi Coffin's in Newport.
    You have a Friend's word." Then I knew.
These weren't *his* slaves. He was Quaker,
    conducting someone else's idea of chattel

on the Underground Railroad to Coffin,
    an ironic name, I think, for a man
who takes the dead and gives them life.
    I did it, though not for pay.

I sized and nailed four oak planks
    and ran a beam between the axles
to gird them up, all the while fearing
    I'd nail those coloreds like Jesus

to the cross of promised redemption.
    A few travelers stopped. I waved
them on, saying everything was in hand,
    and like a good Catholic, I meant

God's hands. It's what I think of
    in church, when I should be tending
to the Mass—that statue of Christ
    holding our globe in His two hands,

the Sacred Heart bursting flame-red
    from His chest. It's what I thought of
when the abscess ate away at Maggie
    till she died young, once pretty,

when Caroline died in childbirth,
    and what I'll think of when life
piddles away through my bad kidneys.
    It's the hands, His heart so big

He could not keep it in His chest—
    these ought to bring me comfort
but don't: How could He make such a world,
    then cradle it delicately in his palms,

and not flinch, or crush us,
    or mourn His fallen handiwork?
Unless it be in our love, as well
    as in our cruelty, we resemble Him.

# Body and Soul

No wonder jays have mulled all day in lilacs,
plotting to cull the first ripe cherry.
The fruit has fattened pink to red
to burgundy, the color of a scab no one
could resist picking, sinking a thumbnail
to taste what gathers in the quarter moon
on near black, as if skin did less to keep
evil out than to hold heaven in. Their
patience is virtue, even of ravenous intent,
for appetite is surely not the worst
we trundled through Eden's clanging gates.
Father Roell swears Adam hid in bushes,
at once ashamed of his nakedness, of Eve's.
Who believes such stories? Startled by
the body's secrets, its casual ruin,
they clothed themselves as if to clothe
temptation. How could they suppose
what mystery an ankle might pose,
what lust in a wrist's curve beneath lace—
all of it trebled by want of fact?
Appetite's a miracle equal to
the loaves and fishes. If not the worst,
it is persistent, that ache for more,
as if in plenitude comes calm. Just say
I'm tempted in the garden, stringing pole
beans and mounding corn. Say a cherry tree
rises flush before those jays, blue darts eyeing
their mark. Suppose all this is as fetching
as my wife's glance as she leaves kitchen
in favor of bath, and say I carry her
a bowl of cherries, resign the rest to jays,
tell me who on earth laments our pleasure?

# Baseball Arrives in Richmond, Indiana

As if winter bore remorse for its game
of hide and seek, I bend down among
the wild iris and purple dame's rocket,
shucking leaves foolish enough to trust
April's disarming come-hither blush.
Winter's parting kiss, my Angela calls it,
as dangerous as all love must be,
why else the budding and blossom and decay?
Which is to say it's noon, I'm drunk,
and none of this has anything to do
with flowers. All morning I drank
with guests, men who fed an arm or leg
to the great beast of the Republic
so hungry for peace it ate itself alive.
These, I fought beside in swamp or woods
or tattered field. These, war spit back,
partial and aggrieved. They were not
as lucky as I, nor as lucky as the dead.
I know it's simple chance that saved me —
not courage or prayer or anything
I might claim as my own. Still I've guilt
enough to keep my distance from the park,
though cheers lift like grackles flapping
through molasses sky: slow to rise,
quick to fall. Always I turn too late
to see what's caused such glee, always
my eye catches the blue clump of amputees
who lean on crutches or hang an empty sleeve,
unable to clap or stand at ease. Four years
after the Great War, I watch our Quaker City
club "do honest battle," as the newspaper says,
with lordly Knightstown. And win.

A peaceful lot, those Quaker men had nothing
of Lincoln's war. They prayed instead,
and God forgive them, kept their hardy limbs.

# Awaiting My Daughter's Suitor

I was thinking of nests: a robin's
stick and mud pack, the horse hair swirl
of the chickadee, that hanging basket
an oriole weaves. How each extends
beyond its use, settled in crook
or stitched to branch long after
autumn has bared them to our view.

All this as innocent and ornamental
as the declamation sunlight gave
upon the young man's face, his arrival
a contrivance of potted chrysanthemums.
The yellow blooms lurched this way and that
as he fumbled free a hand to knock,
and I opened as if it were no reprise,
my youthful bad intentions returned
to haunt me with flowers! For God's sake,
he grew acres of chrysanthemums!

Nothing forever welcomes, not even
the bed you leave to check locks
and stoke the fire, the wind howling
its dire tune as you slide between
chilled sheets, find the quilt wrapped
around your wife, down pillow rebelled
in your absence. I should've known.

This was what my daughter wanted,
why she tended Quaker children,
shined their pots and pans. Why she
scrubbed laundry so rich with the stench

of others she could not look them
in the eye. This was sure to come:
roast beef and steaming *suermoose,*
two growlers of beer from Schneider's tavern,
one less mouth to feed, one more —
"Come down, Josephine. Your Herman is here,"
each footfall the tick of an ominous clock,
the secret clink of dowry in her oak chest.

# Benefit Picnic, Cigar Makers' Strike, August 1884

I'd seen a head or two a club had done with—
    its skin distended across a swollen globe
        of purple-orange and blue, even the holes
            for eyes and nose and mouth puffed shut,

indistinct as those imagination grants
    the full moon, a trick of wishfulness
        that what we see is really human, soon
            to speak to us. Nothing. Not a word.

Still, when I got there, stung by briars
    and low-slung branches, my chest heaving
        for air like the old man I am, when they
            flipped over the body so what was the face

was facing us, I dropped to my knees and retched.
    His black wool jacket, white collar and tie,
        the bit of brown hair not bloodied—all
            belonged to Louis, our son. In the dark

behind the dance floor, while I flounced about
    with his wife, her sallow skin almost pink
        in the gaslight, hired men had yanked him
            from the privy and into the woods, had played

the company tune upon his skull one two three,
    one two three. He'd thought me odd
        to worry so. "This is America!" he'd said,
            as if the words were holy. Now this blessing.

By then the women came running, dress hems
in hand, their petticoats a ghostly presence
hovering above the blond grass. One scream
brought forth a chain of screams receding

like some hysterical human telegraph,
until it reached the bandstand, and music
stopped as a heart in mid-beat, an awful
metaphor I'll admit to, even now.

It's strange what the mind does to keep sane.
I thought to cry, to blubber in public,
was man's worst shame. I refused to give in.
It was one stateliness I'd maintain

for us both, after the stinking mess I'd made
upon seeing the mess they'd made of him.
Instead, I spent the minutes thinking of
what to tell his wife and mother, how he'd

died a martyr for a decent wage, as if
that romantic tale might make his death
less brutal, as if a special heaven
were reserved for union men clubbed

by church-going bosses. It was a stupid lie —
though half-true, and so absorbing in its
own naive way, I hardly heard the voice
behind my head, "Father, I'm all right."

I lurched around to see Louis, clutching
a whisky bottle he and friends had drained
behind the grandstand. Even his drinking
seemed salvation, arisen from the grave

he'd never entered. Such joy I felt
   embracing my drunken Lazarus, such joy
      in my heart, while in my gut a bitter pot
         brewed, bilious and soon to spill—for whose

son was this, splayed dead in the Johnson grass?

# What's Lost as Smoke Is Lost to Sky

We had no mirrors, not one, in the dingy
    upstairs apartment, and no window clean enough
to show a face and hair and eyes at dusk,
    or in candlelight when trees might give

a velveteen backdrop as plush and green
    as any portrait painter's. Though they
say vanity is beauty thorned like a rose,
    it's strange to live behind a face

you can't see as others do, unless reflected,
    shrunken and distant, in the bright iris
of your lover's eyes, and who trusts that?
    I might've had the look that year—working

days on the Whitewater Bridge, all night
    on a house financed with borrowed cash—
the dark-circled, sunken eyes to match
    an immigrant's often sunken spirit,

for eyes, you must've heard, are portals
    to the soul. If my money-lending
neighbor had chanced to look in mine
    some morning after little sleep,

and saw his chicken thief in profile
    against a low slung moon, hens squawking
under each arm, I'm not surprised.
    I suspect my look was hungry enough

to convict the Pope. On Independence Day,
    drunk on bitter ale, Joseph Botter inveighed
against the heavens and chicken-thieving me.
    Neither knife found much flesh.

Trailing spittle, a little blood, the dust
    of a dry year, we limped to the rectory,
where Father patched wounds and took confession.
    By sunrise, Botter took up pen and ink:

*I, Joseph Botter, do hereby declare and say*
    *that in the conversation with William Hale*
*in which I said, 'Bernard Liss stole chickens.'*
    *I had no intention of charging him*

*with the crime of stealing, but spoke the words*
    *in anger, and moreover, that I do not*
*believe Bernard would be or ever was*
    *guilty of such a heinous action.*

Both weak, our anger spent without thought
    of consequence, the way a man will spend
his first paycheck and forget his sore back,
    we left by separate doors. That evening,

Botter counted and sorted eggs by size.
    I folded the sheet of paper, laid it
in a Homestead box in the mantel, then took
    my last three bricks, mortar wet with spit,

and set them in place. In six weeks, our house
    was built. In eight, work bridged the gorge
and Botter rolled west with the National Road,
    past Indianapolis, where another river promised

an emptiness to span with wood and stone.
    Tired of moving, this time we chose to stay,
and in a blank, unforeseen way, chose this place
    to be buried. Though he left without a word,

he left these other words scratched on blue paper,
    each letter pinched tight with anger
for his own loss, with bitterness for mine.
    I ought to burn them, and be done.

# Rooster Saved from the Soup Pot

The house as quiet as the voice
of quiet just before a door slams.
But no door wind-whips shut.

Nothing but brown crickets,
a few peepers, nothing but a hole
in the fabric of sleep,

my face thrust through it
as if through a doorway
opening on a field of wheat.

"Come, come with me,"
I begged of my wife,
though I dared not look back

for fear the door would close.
Behind it, pigweed,
cocklebur, velvetleaf,

shocks of foxtail
and the knee-high milkweed,
its violet blooms as brief,

as fragrant as lilacs.
Each time I hacked them,
they came back, double-stemmed.

Each time thicker,
as if fed by my curses.
This was what I got for hoeing

the prairie's swale belly:
weeds locked about my feet,
tendrils squeezing my thighs

like a vengeful lover.
Wooden-legged, I was a pole
to be climbed, greened over—

but then that rooster's sudden
sore-throated *cockle doodle do*,
and wrenched awake, freed

from the clutches of jopyeweed,
I knew this:
*this* voice I would love.

# What John Chapman Left Behind

Apple blossoms as pink as girls' skin
above lace ruffle, bees drunken
with pollen, dusted yellow and heavy
in still air, a scent so fragrant
it tasted of jam—and me, of course,
all eyes, nose, and mouth, enticed.
It was flesh my flesh could not refuse,
so I let fall my hammer and saw,
rolled up the plans for my neighbor's porch,
and walked the rows he swears
were set by Johnny Appleseed,
charting a death trip up the Whitewater
to the headstreams of the Wabash.
Oh, to be as free as the apple seed man!
Soup pot on head, clad in cast-off
buckskin and coffee sack, he lived
as much outside the world as in it,
as once, given his choice of used brogans
or boots, he took the right of each,
then moved on, his wave as deft
as petal drop.

# St. Andrew's Catholic Men's Choir,
## after Practice, at Blickwedel's Tavern
## and Grocery

It seems the only time we loaf
  or sit awhile, idle as a broken clock,
our calloused hands clasped around
  a mug we think half-empty, half-full,
depending on the price of potatoes,
    how well the pills have stilled the ague
giving our wives the shivers in June.

I've not much to say, and couldn't if I did,
    throat raw from low notes my tenor's baritone
picks and shovels its way down to: even then
    it's like standing chin-deep in a pit,
its walls a crumbling, breathless embrace
    I call low B. I've no gift for song.

Sometimes I've hunkered in Boyce's Woods—
    among the burdock and beggarweed,
sunlight scalloped along its rise
    like the City of God—and listened,
just listened to the chickadee, thrush,
    and blood-red cardinal unleash their flurry
of trills and dips and whistles as if ecstatic

in prayer. In sober moments I knew it was
    more alarm than prayer, something like:
"Beware of the bearded man on bent knee,"
    though it was enticing to think that song
could stick with me as efficiently
    as the burrs I plucked from pants and sleeves,
spreading weeds instead of the Word.

One morning I shed envy as a snake sheds
    old skin, my head the first to let go.
Mist rose through hickory, oak, black locust,
    and I leaned against the wood's only pawpaw,
feasting on its fleshy fruit, the Indiana banana.
    Of a sudden a thunderous pounding,
the tree shook, and pawpaws cascaded down

upon me. Shielding my eyes, I saw him:
    a great pileated woodpecker, his tufted head
a blur of red intention. Halting his work,
    he spied me, a brother of hammer and wood,
and gave the curious cackle that is his call,
    his voice no better than mine.
I knew then the song meant more than the singer.

Looking back, I'd overlooked that truth
    like a lazy mushroom hunter too foolish
to paw beneath spring's wet leaves. I'd met
    my wife at choir, her loveliness less of flesh
than the notion philosophers call *essence*,
    what other men refuse to name for fear
they'll destroy, or understand, it—

either way it's gone, irretrievable
    as first-ploughed prairie, its departure
attended by that ripping sound soil makes
    as a blade cleaves its weave of big bluestem,
coneflower, chickory and more. Lord knows,
    these women have little to show for it:

stooped backs, breasts that sag from their
    intended use, a gold ring the only thing
that shines besides their blue-gray eyes,
    bright with slant light sluiced through

glazed glass, children too young for lager
   circled and shimmering at their feet.

What moved my Angela to leave her family,
   cross a roiling sea in the dank belly
of a cargo ship we feared would sink
   at any hour, it leaked so; and once here,
why chance river and canal, the wagon
   we shared with three pigs on route to slaughter,
our last stretch on foot from Centerville,

only to arrive to nothing: no home, no friends,
   no promise of work better than word of mouth?
It's folly to ask such questions.
   They lead to truth or lies, and both can blind.
All right, maybe it's only a drunken wondering,
   only the pitiful inclination of a happy man
to tempt God, to eye His red-dressed lady Fate,

to ask of Him who spared me the king's wrath,
   fed me black bread from secret hands
when every potato in the county had blighted,
   He who must've been happily drunk to set me
down among Germans, in flat-land Indiana,
   with the Road and all its bridges and mills,
banks and Quaker merchant homes to build,

with a wife who doesn't mind the winters
   and takes a lager on special occasions,
with a house I built and family to make it home,
   with a tin lunch bucket, dented and long past shine,
which, once emptied, a nickel will fill with beer,
   to ask of Him, in a hoarse voice: Why bless me?

# 3  The Call

# Authorial Distance

It's a kind of ambush,
that rush of meadowlarks
clustered among forsythia,
blooms awash with feverish bees
droning, droning, droning.
A kind of ambush, this flush
of yellow his dog sets off
as though light were wing and petal
and nothing was born to die —
two notions as fitful as joy
or hope, words owning an O
wide enough to slip his soul in,
house key in the lock of faith.
April, and White River's as turbid
as what his infant son hacked up.
Rose water, stump water, breath of cat,
nothing cleared the boy's lungs.
Now baptism seems an everlasting
bargain. This morning I watch him
from a distance he can't imagine,
and you watch too, maybe reading
in a chair whose springs creak
to let you in, the walls around you
as white as this 80 lb. stock.
Maybe you're wondering what you're
doing in this poem. Maybe you're
bemused because this violates
our shared distance, though space
is only another name for time
and neither of us has much of that.
So stand here next to me. As near
as you can bear. Turn your ear

toward my lips, brave my stale breath,
and I'll confess this man we're watching
doesn't see the yellow meadowlarks
among arcs of forsythia; doesn't notice
the dog, black against purple sky.
These facts of my life I've lent
to his, 140 years after he signed
his son's death certificate,
which I'll unfold and read to you:
"Consumption." All I know of both
of them I carry shoe-boxed, mailed
to me as last of kin by neighbors
of a great-aunt I hardly knew,
the German stamps peeled off
as payment for their trouble.
Here hold these—his few letters,
a note absolving chicken thievery,
the calfskin deed scavenged from trash.
All of it musty, liver-spotted,
brittle as eggshell in your pink
and open palms. You must be thinking
what dross a life, once spent, is.
What wild, rampant pleasures
reduced to paper, to dust.
You must be thinking what pitiful
account each of us leaves,
as I will leave these wings
and petals that fulgurate
beneath a cluster of thunderheads,
my own pitiful account of this
febrile rush I feel, box in hand,
ambushed by the answering machine's
yellow eye, eye, eye—
as if, though gone,
I had not missed his call.

## Illinois Poetry Series
*Laurence Lieberman, Editor*

History Is Your Own Heartbeat
*Michael S. Harper* (1971)

The Foreclosure
*Richard Emil Braun* (1972)

The Scrawny Sonnets and Other
Narratives
*Robert Bagg* (1973)

The Creation Frame
*Phyllis Thompson* (1973)

To All Appearances: Poems New
and Selected
*Josephine Miles* (1974)

The Black Hawk Songs
*Michael Borich* (1975)

Nightmare Begins Responsibility
*Michael S. Harper* (1975)

The Wichita Poems
*Michael Van Walleghen* (1975)

Images of Kin: New and
Selected Poems
*Michael S. Harper* (1977)

Poems of the Two Worlds
*Frederick Morgan* (1977)

Cumberland Station
*Dave Smith* (1977)

Tracking
*Virginia R. Terris* (1977)

Riversongs
*Michael Anania* (1978)

On Earth as It Is
*Dan Masterson* (1978)

Coming to Terms
*Josephine Miles* (1979)

Death Mother and Other Poems
*Frederick Morgan* (1979)

Goshawk, Antelope
*Dave Smith* (1979)

Local Men
*James Whitehead* (1979)

Searching the Drowned Man
*Sydney Lea* (1980)

With Akhmatova at the Black Gates
*Stephen Berg* (1981)

Dream Flights
*Dave Smith* (1981)

More Trouble with the Obvious
*Michael Van Walleghen* (1981)

The American Book of the Dead
*Jim Barnes* (1982)

The Floating Candles
*Sydney Lea* (1982)

Northbook
*Frederick Morgan* (1982)

Collected Poems, 1930–83
*Josephine Miles* (1983)

The River Painter
*Emily Grosholz* (1984)

Healing Song for the Inner Ear
*Michael S. Harper* (1984)

The Passion of the Right-Angled Man
*T. R. Hummer* (1984)

Dear John, Dear Coltrane
*Michael S. Harper* (1985)

Poems from the Sangamon
*John Knoepfle* (1985)

In It
*Stephen Berg* (1986)

The Ghosts of Who We Were
*Phyllis Thompson* (1986)

Moon in a Mason Jar
*Robert Wrigley* (1986)

Lower-Class Heresy
*T. R. Hummer* (1987)

Poems: New and Selected
*Frederick Morgan* (1987)

Furnace Harbor: A Rhapsody of
the North Country
*Philip D. Church* (1988)

Bad Girl, with Hawk
*Nance Van Winckel* (1988)

Blue Tango
*Michael Van Walleghen* (1989)

Eden
*Dennis Schmitz* (1989)

Waiting for Poppa at the
Smithtown Diner
*Peter Serchuk* (1990)

Great Blue
*Brendan Galvin* (1990)

What My Father Believed
*Robert Wrigley* (1991)

Something Grazes Our Hair
*S. J. Marks* (1991)

Walking the Blind Dog
*G. E. Murray* (1992)

The Sawdust War
*Jim Barnes* (1992)

The God of Indeterminacy
*Sandra McPherson* (1993)

Off-Season at the Edge of the World
*Debora Greger* (1994)

Counting the Black Angels
*Len Roberts* (1994)

Oblivion
*Stephen Berg* (1995)

To Us, All Flowers Are Roses
*Lorna Goodison* (1995)

Honorable Amendments
*Michael S. Harper* (1995)

Points of Departure
*Miller Williams* (1995)

Dance Script with Electric Ballerina
*Alice Fulton* (reissue, 1996)

To the Bone: New and
Selected Poems
*Sydney Lea* (1996)

Floating on Solitude
*Dave Smith* (3-volume reissue, 1996)

Bruised Paradise
*Kevin Stein* (1996)

Walt Whitman Bathing
*David Wagoner* (1996)

## National Poetry Series

Eroding Witness
*Nathaniel Mackey* (1985)
Selected by Michael S. Harper

Palladium
*Alice Fulton* (1986)
Selected by Mark Strand

Cities in Motion
*Sylvia Moss* (1987)
Selected by Derek Walcott

The Hand of God and a Few
Bright Flowers
*William Olsen* (1988)
Selected by David Wagoner

The Great Bird of Love
*Paul Zimmer* (1989)
Selected by William Stafford

Stubborn
*Roland Flint* (1990)
Selected by Dave Smith

The Surface
*Laura Mullen* (1991)
Selected by C. K. Williams

The Dig
*Lynn Emanuel* (1992)
Selected by Gerald Stern

My Alexandria
*Mark Doty* (1993)
Selected by Philip Levine

The High Road to Taos
*Martin Edmunds* (1994)
Selected by Donald Hall

Theater of Animals
*Samn Stockwell* (1995)
Selected by Louise Glück

The Broken World
*Marcus Cafagña* (1996)
Selected by Yusef Komunyakaa

## Other Poetry Volumes

*Local Men* and *Domains*
James Whitehead (1987)

Her Soul beneath the Bone: Women's
Poetry on Breast Cancer
*Edited by Leatrice Lifshitz* (1988)

Days from a Dream Almanac
*Dennis Tedlock* (1990)

Working Classics: Poems on
Industrial Life
*Edited by Peter Oresick and
Nicholas Coles* (1990)

Hummers, Knucklers, and Slow Curves:
Contemporary Baseball Poems
*Edited by Don Johnson* (1991)

The Double Reckoning of
Christopher Columbus
*Barbara Helfgott Hyett* (1992)

Selected Poems
*Jean Garrigue* (1992)

New and Selected Poems, 1962–92
*Laurence Lieberman* (1993)

*The Dig* and *Hotel Fiesta*
Lynn Emanuel (1994)

For a Living: The Poetry of Work
*Edited by Nicholas Coles and
Peter Oresick* (1995)

The Tracks We Leave: Poems on
Endangered Wildlife of
North America
*Barbara Helfgott Hyett*